ANCIENT GREEK DESIGNS

MARTY NOBLE

DOVER PUBLICATIONS, INC.
Mineola, New York

Bibliographical Note

Ancient Greek Designs is a new work, first published by Dover Publications, Inc., in 2000.

DOVER *Pictorial Archive* SERIES

Library of Congress Cataloging-in-Publication Data

Noble, Mary, 1948–
    Ancient Greek designs / Marty Noble.
        p. cm. — (Dover pictorial archive series)
    ISBN 0-486-41228-8 (pbk.)
    1. Decoration and ornament—Greece—Themes, motives. 2. Decoration and ornament, Ancient—Greece—Themes, motives. I. Title. II. Series.
NK1230 .N63 2000
745.4'4938—dc21

00-034638

Manufactured in the United States of America
Dover Publications, Inc., 31 East 2nd Street, Mineola, N.Y. 11501

PUBLISHER'S NOTE

This compact collection of Ancient Greek designs includes works created between the sixteenth and the first centuries B.C. The early pieces are from the civilizations of the Aegean Sea, including settlements on both the Greek islands and mainland. The city of Mycenae became the center of this culture, much as Athens was in later years. During this period, the end of the Bronze Age, Aegean art owed more to the older civilizations of the Near East than it did to native Greek or to other European influences. But this changed after the invasion of the Dorians, from the north, and the subsequent decline of the Mycenaeans. After a period that left only fragmentary evidence of its existence, appropriately called the Greek Dark Ages, the great city-states came to prominence in the eighth century B.C. Despite periodic wars and turmoil, these localities, many of them with democratically elected rulers, provided an environment in which the arts could flourish. In particular, Athens in the age of Pericles (fifth century) experienced a period of unprecedented creativity. Many of the works illustrated in this book were produced during and just after this period, which spanned most of the fifth and fourth centuries B.C.

Much of the Ancient Greeks' art was based on images of their early history, which is called mythology today but which was as real to the Greeks as King Arthur is to the English or the Pilgrim fathers are to Americans. The images and designs were used to enhance everyday objects, including domestic items, such as pottery and clothing, and implements of war, such as helmets, shields, and the like. Buildings and monuments were also embellished with artistic creations. The early pages of this book contain drawings of works in bas relief on marble or common stone. Then there are a number of figures, both humans and gods, and a group of painted vases, plates, cups, and other vessels. In the final pages are drawings of jewelry and musical instruments, followed by examples of Greek ornamentation. Studying this collection, one can see why critics past and present have been struck by the "extreme simplicity and thorough rationality," the "idealism and ethical purpose," evident in the art of Ancient Greece.

Mycenaean seals, embellished with figures of animals. Seals were a practical way of identification and security in the ancient world; 15th century B.C.

Votive relief showing the deification of Homer; 2nd century B.C.

ABOVE, LEFT: Metope, from the Temple of Zeus at Olympia. ABOVE, RIGHT: Caryatid, from the south porch of the Erechtheum, Athens; c.410 B.C. CENTER: Lid of a gilt silver box, found near Tarentum; late 2nd century, B.C. BELOW: Amazonomachy, marble, Temple of Apollo, Bassae; c.410 B.C.

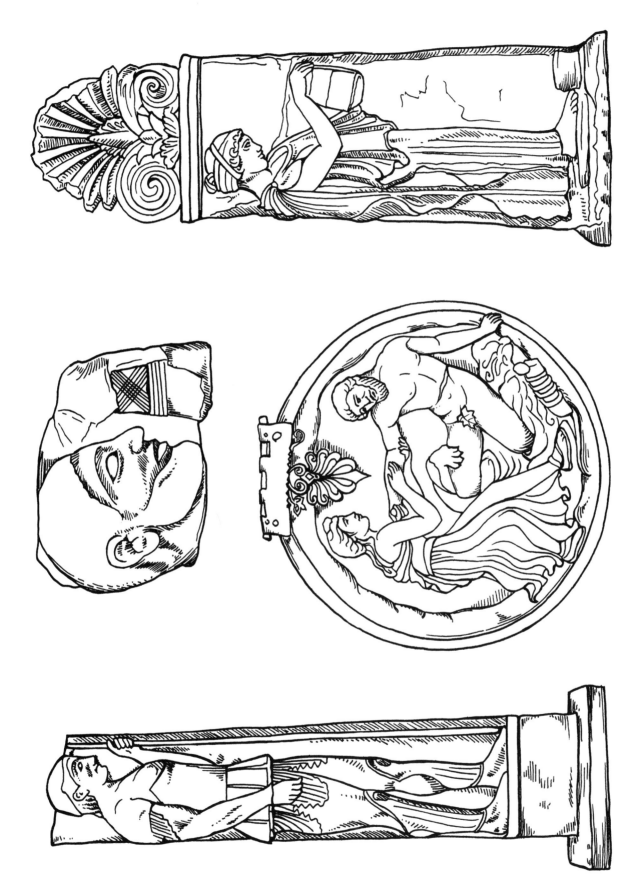

LEFT: Gravestone of Aristion, Attica; 510 B.C. TOP: Fragment of gravestone, Athens; 510 B.C. BOTTOM: Bronze mirror cover, Elis (Eleia); 5th century B.C. RIGHT: Gravestone of a girl, from a Greek island; 450 B.C.

7

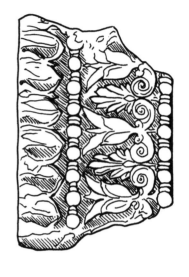

ABOVE, LEFT: Centauromachy, metope, from the Parthenon, Athens, 447–442 B.C. BELOW, LEFT: Relief, young athletes, base of a statue marking a grave, Athens; c.510 B.C. ABOVE, RIGHT: Clay plaque, Demeter and Dionysus, Loqri; 460 B.C. BELOW, RIGHT: Decorative border, from a frieze on a Treasury, Delphi; late 6th century, B.C.

ABOVE: "Amazon Leaping to Her Death," marble relief, from a shipwreck off Piraeus.
BELOW: Archaizing relief, "Dionysus with Three Seasons"; 1st century B.C.

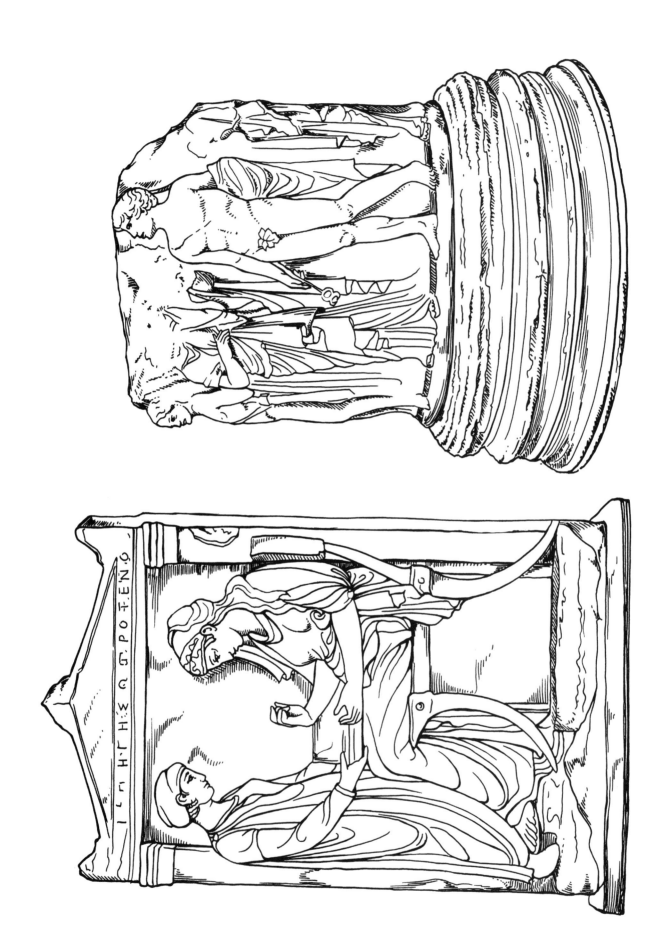

LEFT: "Hegeso and a Servant," Attic grave stele; 400 B.C.

RIGHT: "Thanatos, Alcestis and Hermes," column drum, carved in relief, Temple of Artemis, Ephesus.

Fragments from the "Procession of Alexander," bas relief, as rendered c.1800 by Bertel Thorwaldsen.

ABOVE: Horsemen troop along the Panathenaic Way, section of frieze, Parthenon.
BELOW: "Alexander in a Battle," tomb of Alexander the Great; c.310 B.C.

LEFT: Young warrior in battle regalia, drawing on fictile vase.
ABOVE, RIGHT: Greek helmet. BELOW, RIGHT: Theban shield.

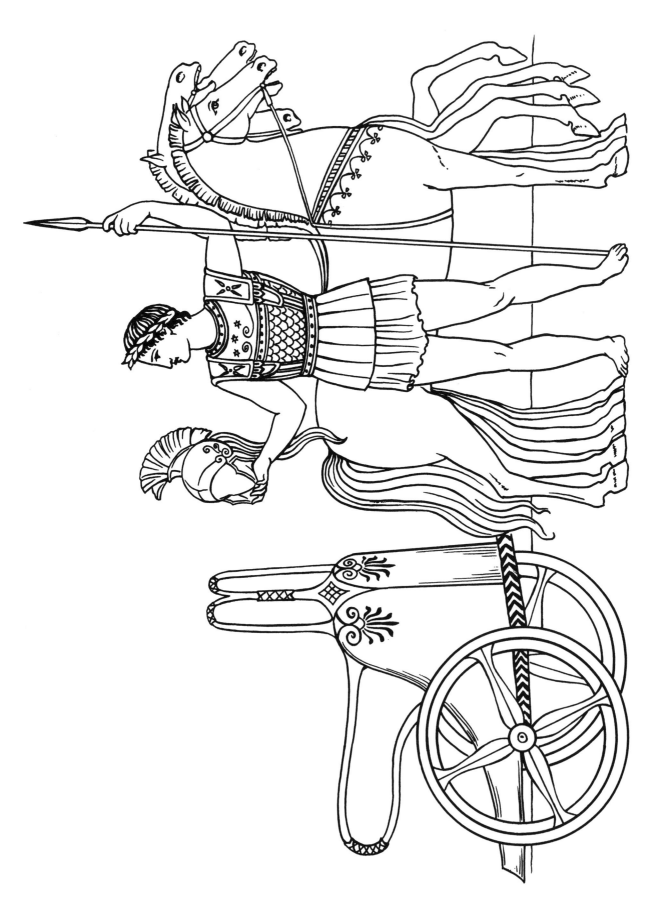

Victorious warrior standing next to his chariot.

LEFT: Shields. ABOVE, RIGHT: Scabbard and helmet. BELOW, RIGHT: Chariot with six-spoked wheel.

15

ABOVE: Helmets. BELOW, LEFT: Scabbard. BELOW, RIGHT: Chariot with four-spoked wheel.

Warriors poised for combat, both wearing greaves (leg armor). The soldier on the left is covered from neck to waist by a cuirass, while the other man's armor protects only his neck and shoulders.

Zeus, as depicted on a vase.

Bacchanalian on a couch, holding a thyrsus in his left hand; by his side are a candelabrum (left) and a tripod (right).

Grecian women, dressed in the old style, separated by a tympanum, or drum, and seated on a platform decorated with a typical Greek border design.

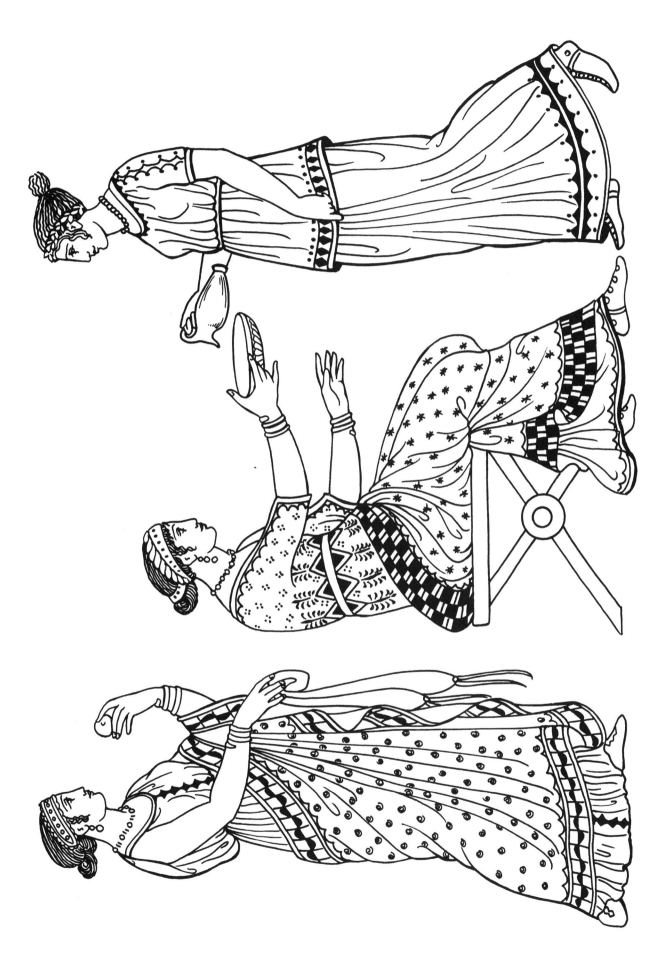

Grecian women, as depicted on a fictile vase.

21

Woman holding ceremonial rod, in drawing
with typical Greek ornamentation in the four corners.

Woman playing the *aulos*, or double oboes, with Bacchante (devotee of Bacchus)
sounding the *crotala*; probably 5th century B.C.

Bacchante with rod of sesame in crook of elbow, holding laurel wreath above amphora.

Woman seated, shaded by an umbrella. Just below her chair is a crafted box,
probably for personal toiletries, with a decorated chest in the foreground.

ABOVE, LEFT AND RIGHT: Ornate headdresses. CENTER: Woman as depicted on a fictile vase.
BORDERS: Traditional ornaments.

Two different depictions of the goddess Athena.

Bacchante, cradling thyrsus under left arm.

ABOVE: Bacchanalian *rhytons* (drinking horns).
BELOW: Drawing on a cup made in Laconia, with representations of two Titans, Atlas and Prometheus.

ABOVE: Vase on ornamental stand. BELOW: Red figure plate, from Tarentum, "Heracles Bringing Cerberus from the Underworld"; early 4th century B.C.

LEFT: Plate, with drawing of Zeus accepting an offering. RIGHT: Jug.

LEFT: Red figure plate, "Oedipus Questioning the Sphinx"; c.500 B.C. RIGHT: Toilet box, "Aphrodite Arriving at Cyprus"; c.475 B.C.

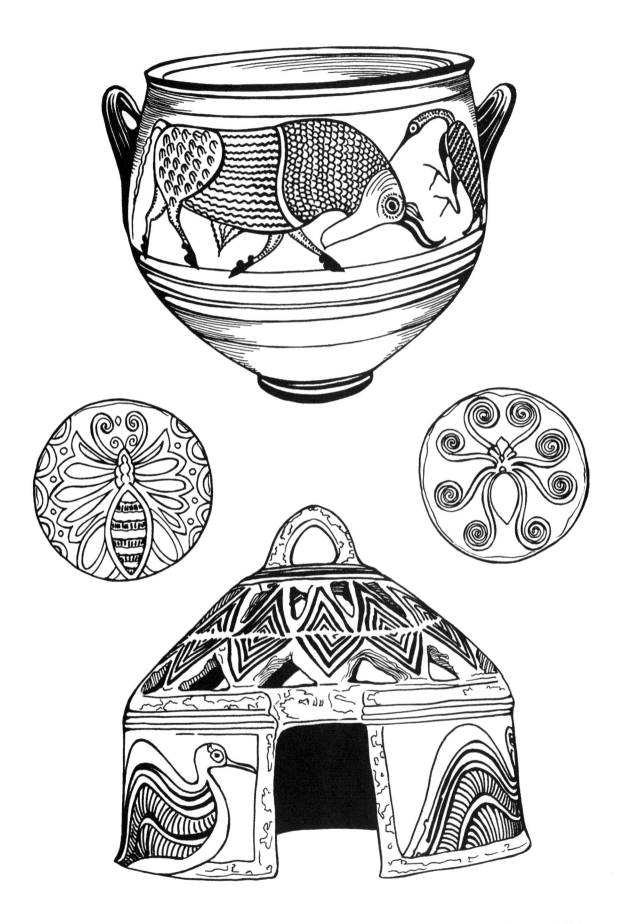

ABOVE: *Krater,* terra cotta with glaze painting, Mycenae, 13th century B.C. MIDDLE: Decorated disks, used to fasten clothing, Mycenae; 6th century B.C. BELOW: Cover for an incense burner, terra cotta, Palaikastro, Crete; 13th century B.C.

33

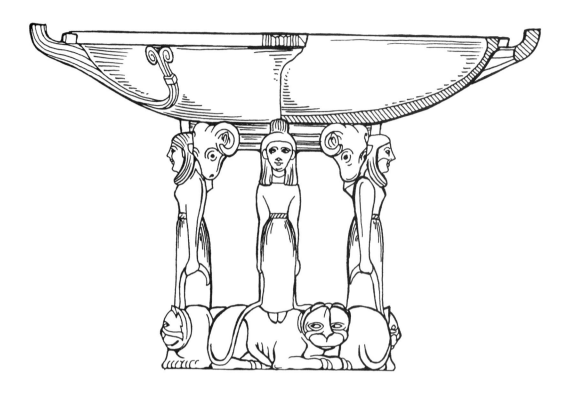

Restored drawings. ABOVE: *Perirrhanterion* basin, from sanctuary of Poseidon, near Corinth;
a rare sculpture of women from the late 7th century B.C. BELOW: Restored drawing of a chalice made in
Chios for export; c.560 B.C. Found in the ruins of an ancient Greek colony in Libya.

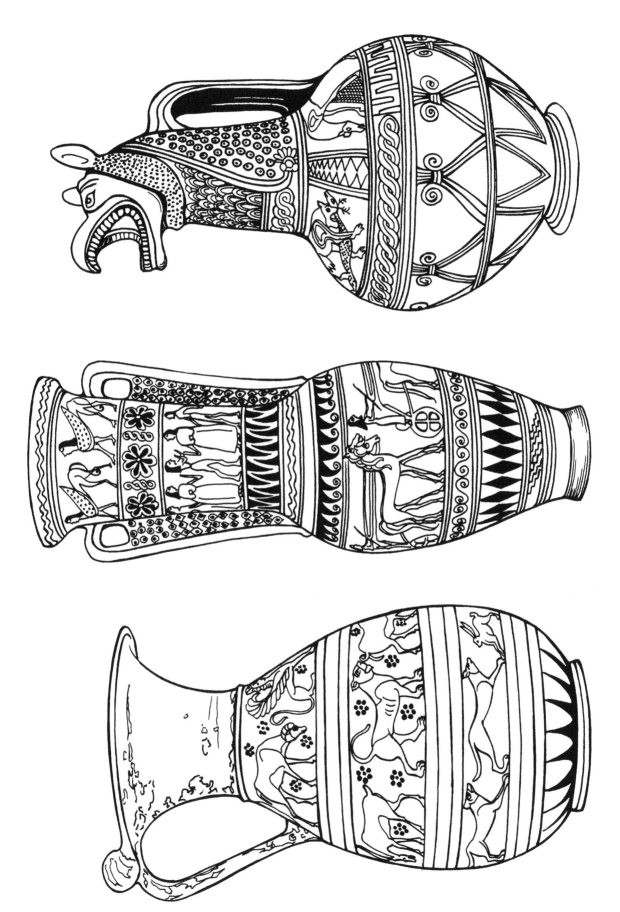

LEFT: Protocorinthian *olpe*, jug decorated with friezes of animals and sphinxes, in the black figure technique with characteristic dot rosettes; c.640 B.C.
MIDDLE: Protoattic vase, decorated with horse-drawn chariots, sphinxes, and dancers; c.690 B.C.
RIGHT: Griffin jug from Aegina, painted in the Cyclades; c.675 B.C.

35

Attic vase, "Death of Actaeon"; c.460 B.C.

Black-figured amphora, "Dionysus and the Maenads"; thought to be the work
of the Amassis painter, c.530 B.C.

Bacchanalians, painted on a fictive vase

CENTER: Bacchanalians, painted on vase with medallion handles.
SIDES & BOTTOM: Ornamental borders.

39

Black-figured amphora, "Alexander's Procession."

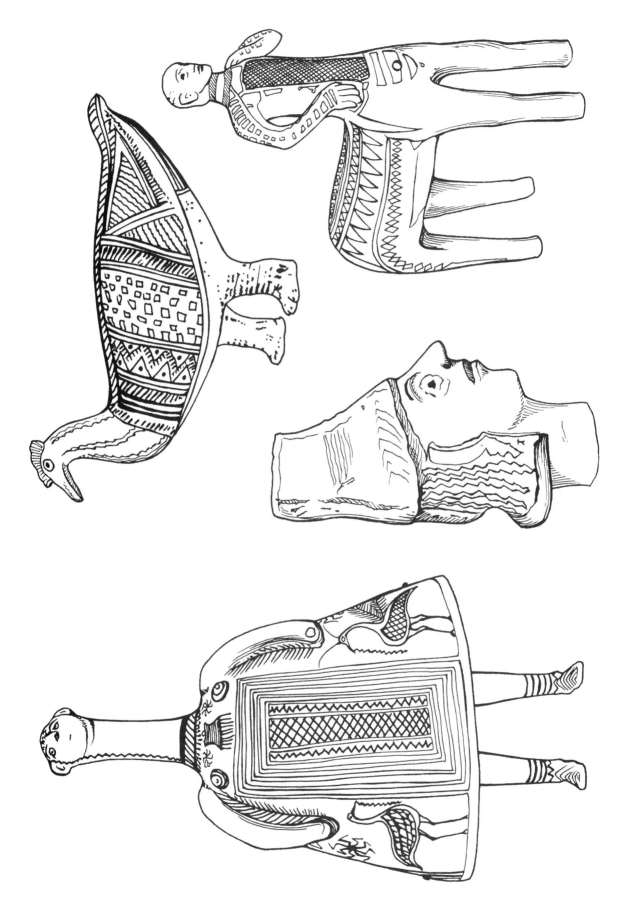

LEFT: Clay figure of woman, Boeotia; c.700 B.C. ABOVE, RIGHT: Terra cotta bird figure, with glaze paint, from Athens; c.750 B.C. BELOW, RIGHT: Clay figure, centaur, from Lefkandi, Euoboea; c.900 B.C. CENTER: Clay head of a helmeted warrior, from temple at Amyclae, near Sparta; c.700 B.C.

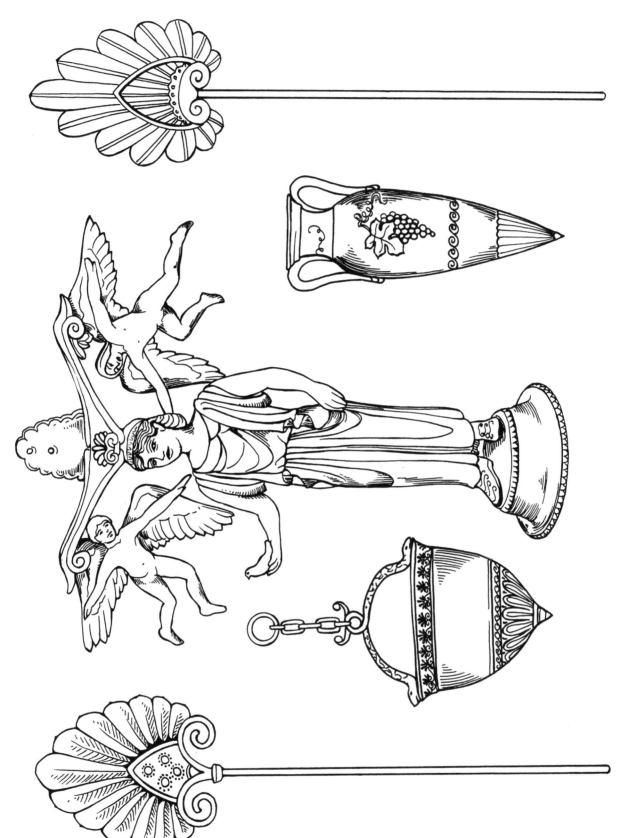

LEFT & RIGHT: Fans, made of feathers and leaves. CENTER: "Aphrodite and Erotes," bronze support for a mirror, c.480 B.C. Flanking the bronze are a lamp (left) and an amphora (right).

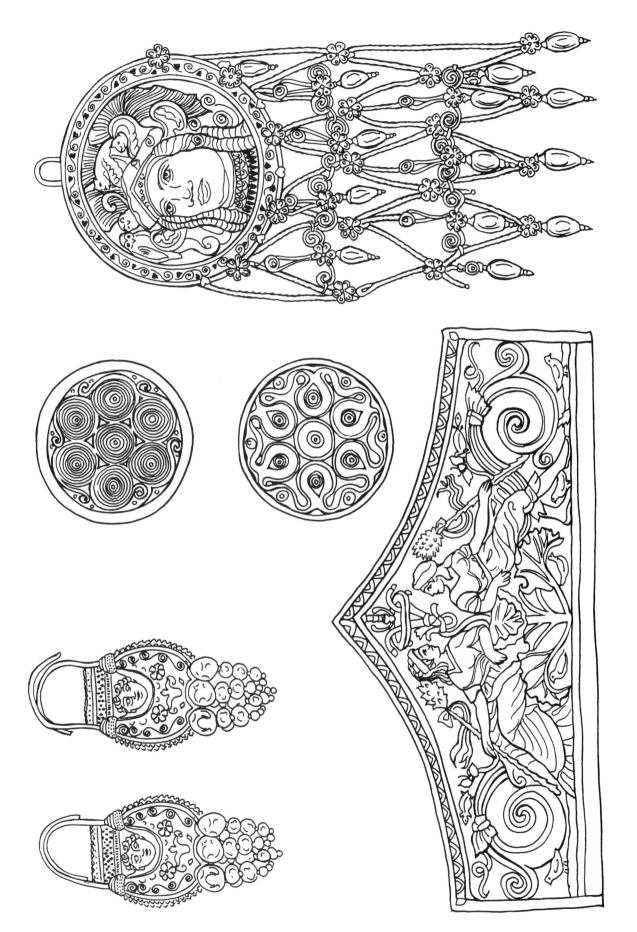

LEFT: Gold earrings, from Tarentum; c.330 B.C. CENTER: Ornamental disks, used to fasten clothing, Mycenae; 6th century B.C. RIGHT: Gold pendant, with head of the Athena Parthenos, Athens; 4th century B.C. BELOW, LEFT: Gold diadem, from the northeastern Aegean Sea; 330–300 B.C.

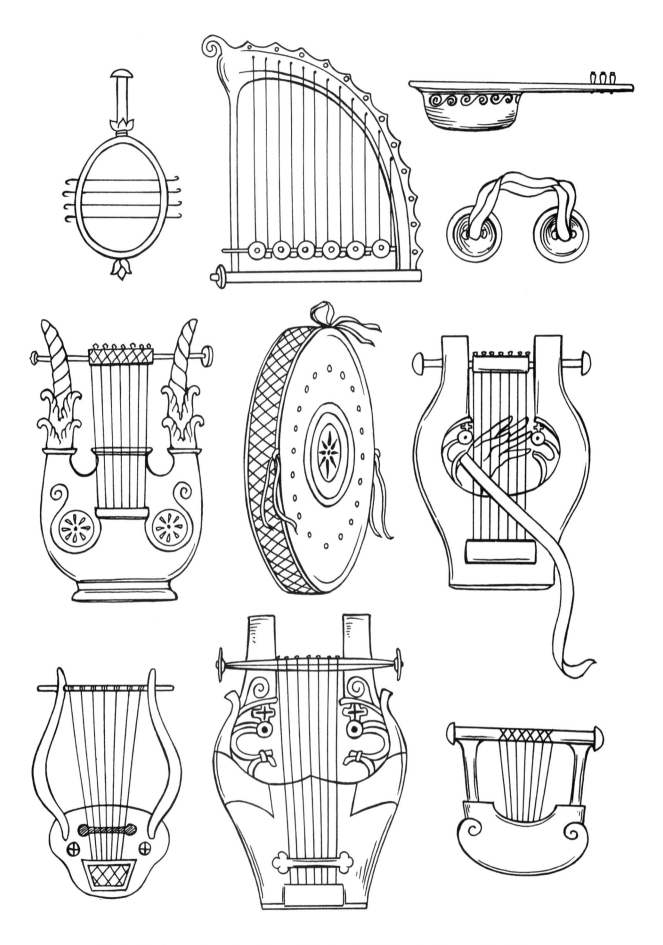

Musical instruments: various forms of the lyre, including the *Lyra* and the *kithara*,
and two common percussion instuments

Ornamentation

Ornamentation

Ornamentation

Detail from a frieze, great altar of Zeus at Pergamum; c.180 B.C. Athena seizes a
winged giant by his hair as he is attacked by a snake.